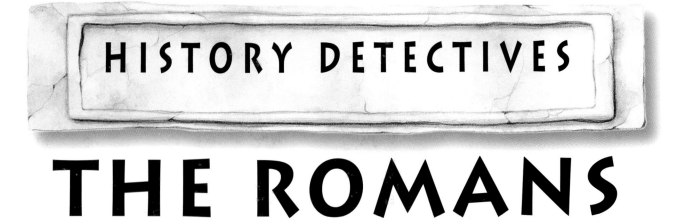

HISTORY DETECTIVES

THE ROMANS

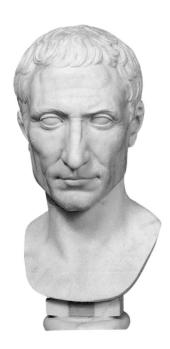

HISTORY DETECTIVES

THE ROMANS

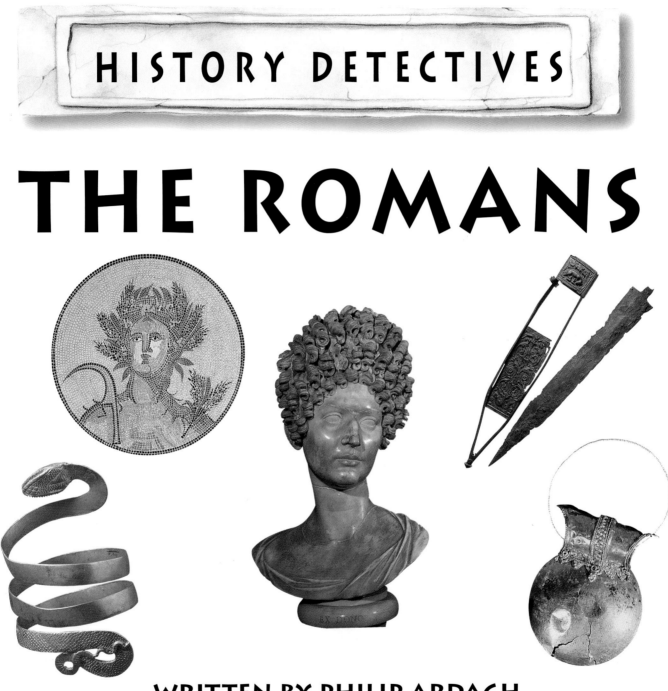

WRITTEN BY PHILIP ARDAGH
ILLUSTRATED BY COLIN KING

PETER BEDRICK BOOKS
NTC/Contemporary Publishing Group
NEW YORK

First published in the United States of America in 2000 by
Peter Bedrick Books
a division of NTC/Contemporary Publishing Group
4255 West Touhy Avenue
Lincolnwood (Chicago), Illinois, 60712-1975, USA

ISBN 0-87226-631-1

Printed in Singapore

The publishers would like to thank the following for their permission to use the photographic material reproduced in this book.

a = above, b = below, c = centre, l = left, r = right

opening page: Pio-Clementino Museum, Vatican, Rome/Scala; title page: National Museum, Naples/Scala, Lesley and Roy Adkins Picture Library,
Capitoline Museum, Rome/ Photo Resources/Mike Dixon; Museum of London; Ancient Art & Architecture Collection; contents page: Vatican, Rome/Scala;
8: Roy Rainford/Robert Harding Picture Library; 9a: C. Gascoigne/Robert Harding Picture Library; 9b: Ancient Art & Architecture Collection; 10a: Pio-
Clementino Museum, Vatican, Rome/Scala; 10b: Vatican, Rome/Scala; 11a: Museum of London; 11b: British Museum/Michael Holford; 13a: Capitoline
Museum, Rome/Scala; 13b: Ancient Art & Architecture Collection; 15a: Photo Resources; 15b: British Museum/Michael Holford; 17a: House of the Vettii,
Pompeii/Scala; 17b: Photo Resources; 19a: Roman Villa, Piazza Armerina/Scala; 19b: National Trust Photographic Library/Ian Shaw; 21a: Robert Harding
Picture Library; 21b: Archaeological Museum, Foligno/Scala; 23a: Capitoline Museum, Rome/Scala; 23b: Photo Resources; 25a: Photo Resources; 25b:
Uffizi, Florence/Scala; 27: Lesley and Roy Adkins Picture Library; 29a: Museum of London; 29b: Ancient Art & Architecture Collection; 31a: Museum of
London; 31b: Ancient Art & Architecture Collection; 33a: Museum of London; 33b: British Museum/Photo Resources; 35a: Capitoline Museum, Rome/Photo
Resources; 35b: National Museum, Naples/Scala; 37a & b: Ancient Art & Architecture Collection; 38a: Photo Resources; 38b: Ancient Art & Architecture
Collection; 39a: Ancient Art & Architecture Collection; 39b: Photo Resources; 40a: National Museum, Rome/Photo Resources; 40b: Ancient Art &
Architecture; 41a: G Gascoigne/Robert Harding Picture Library; 41b: Adam Woolfitt/Robert Harding Picture Library.

CONTENTS

THE ROMANS

The first Romans got their name from the city of Rome. They originally came from a tribe called the Latins. Rome is in what we now call Italy. (You can find out how the city got its name on page 13.)

The city of Rome was set up in the 8th century BC and became a republic about 200 years later. The Republic was governed by people elected by the Romans instead of being ruled by kings or emperors. Those elected were called senators and they ruled in the parliament called the Senate.

WAR

In the early years, Rome wasn't the great power it later became. The Romans had to fight to survive. They had many enemies, including the Gauls (who came from Gallia, which we now know as France).

Another great enemy was Hannibal from Carthage. In the Punic Wars he led 35,000 men and 37 elephants across the snowy Alps to attack the Roman armies in 218BC. 10,000 men and 36 of the elephants died along the way.

Although he had many victories against the Romans, Hannibal never managed to conquer Rome itself. Over time, the Romans spread their control right across Europe.

The Roman Empire under Emperor Trajan.

Caledonia
BRITANNIA
Germania Inferior
Belgica
Lugdunensis
Germania Superior
GALLIA (FRE
Rhaet
Aquitania
Narbonensis
Tarraconensis
HISPANIA
Lusitania
Baetica
Mediterranean Sea
Sardini
Tingitana
MAURETANIA
Numidia

Slaves often fought as gladiators in the Colosseum in Rome.

Ancient carvings give clues to everyday Roman life.

Many ancient Roman buildings are still standing today.

THE BIRTH OF AN EMPIRE

After the death of Julius Caesar, the leader of the Senate, in 44BC, there was disagreement over who should lead Rome. You can read about this on pages 10 and 11. Then, in 27BC, Caesar's adopted son, Octavian, became the first emperor, Augustus. He was given complete power and did not have to be elected by the people. Rome was therefore no longer a republic but an empire. This empire grew and grew, and was at its biggest under the Emperor Trajan who ruled from AD98 to AD117.

DIFFERENT LIVES

Under Roman rule, life was very good for some people and terrible for others. Roman citizens could gain wealth and have fun, while others were often harshly treated, or even became slaves.

While the well-off could eat seven-course banquets, many others relied on bread to stay alive. Riots often broke out if the ships carrying grain, to make bread, didn't arrive from Egypt on time.

It was difficult to keep command over so many conquered countries. Over time, the Roman Empire lost its power. It was too big to control, and was split into groups. By the 5th century AD it had fallen. The Roman Empire was over.

9

DISCOVERY

This amazingly life-like marble bust is of Julius Caesar. Roman emperors later took the name "Caesar" and used it as a title. Some other countries called their leaders "Kaiser," "Tsar" or "Czar" which are also titles based on Caesar's name.

Over 80 statues of Octavian were erected once he became Augustus, and that was just in Rome! This is the most famous one of all. It's called the Prima Porta after the place where it was found.

FAMOUS NAMES

Julius Caesar (c.100BC–44BC) was probably the most famous of all Romans. He was voted ruler of the Senate for life. He was very popular with ordinary Romans because he used his power to make life better for them. He became unpopular with the senators because he stopped asking their advice before doing anything. Finally, Caesar's friend Brutus, and another senator called Cassius, plotted with a group of people to murder Julius Caesar. They hoped that someone else would then be elected to the Senate to take Caesar's place. This never happened and, in fact, the death of Caesar meant the death of the Republic.

THE FIRST EMPEROR

With Caesar dead, many of the army generals tried to take his place—this led to years of civil war. Finally the Senate agreed to give overall power to Octavian, Caesar's adopted son. When he became Rome's first emperor in 27BC, he was given the new name of Augustus.

Before then, Octavian had a friend called Mark Anthony, but when Anthony fell in love with Cleopatra, Queen of Egypt, they ended up on opposite sides. Octavian defeated Cleopatra, and Egypt became a Roman province in 30BC.

LITTLE BOOTS

Like Octavian, Emperor Gaius (AD12–41) was also better known by another name. He got the nickname Caligula from his choice of footwear, and this is how he is best remembered! *Caligae* is the Latin word for "little boots." Caligula was emperor of Rome from AD37–AD41 and was very cruel and probably insane. He tried to have his favorite horse made a consul — one of the most important jobs in government! Like Caesar, he too was murdered. The culprits were the Praetorian Guard, a special group of soldiers who were supposed to protect him.

ROME BURNS

After Caligula, Claudius became emperor and, after Claudius, there was Emperor Nero (AD37–68). Nero is famous for "fiddling while Rome burned." He actually played the lyre not the fiddle (fiddles hadn't been invented). There is a legend that Nero himself set fire to Rome so that he could build a new city. Of course, he couldn't admit to this so he blamed it on the Christians. A bigger, better Rome was built but, in the end, Nero — who'd had his own mother murdered — killed himself.

ONE GOD

The Christians were punished by the Romans throughout most of Roman history, along with the Jews and other groups who would not worship the Roman gods. When a man called Constantine (c.AD274–AD337) became emperor in AD324, all this changed. He moved the control of the empire from Rome to Byzantium, which he then renamed Constantinople. (This city is now known as Istanbul.) Constantine was a Christian, so under him Christianity spread. By the end of the 4th century AD it had become the state religion.

DISCOVERY

Caligula got his nickname from the boots he wore as a boy. These, more elegant, Roman shoes were found in London.

Caesar first invaded Britain with a small force in 55BC, but Claudius — who became emperor after Caligula — led the all-out conquest of "Britannia" in AD43.

This brass coin, called a *sestertius*, shows the head of the power-hungry Emperor Nero. Nero loved gladiator fights and chariot races so much that he raised taxes to pay for more.

THE CITY OF ROME

No one knows for sure when Rome became a city. It grew from a group of separate villages on seven hills, by the River Tiber. According to legend, however, Rome was set up in 753BC, which is probably about the time it really became a city. Rome was on the most important trade routes, giving the Romans a chance to buy and sell goods from all over the world. After a fire in AD64, the city was rebuilt on an even bigger and grander scale, spreading to both sides of the river.

Rome became the biggest and most fantastic city in the ancient world. As well as many fabulous public buildings — everything from theaters and temples to bath houses — there were grand homes for the rich, and shabby, bad quality houses for the poor. At its height, the city housed over a million people. Many parts were very overcrowded. There were even traffic jams.

Forum of Augustus, one of a number of meeting places where people met to talk and trade

Palace of the Emperor Augustus

Circus Maximus, a chariot race track

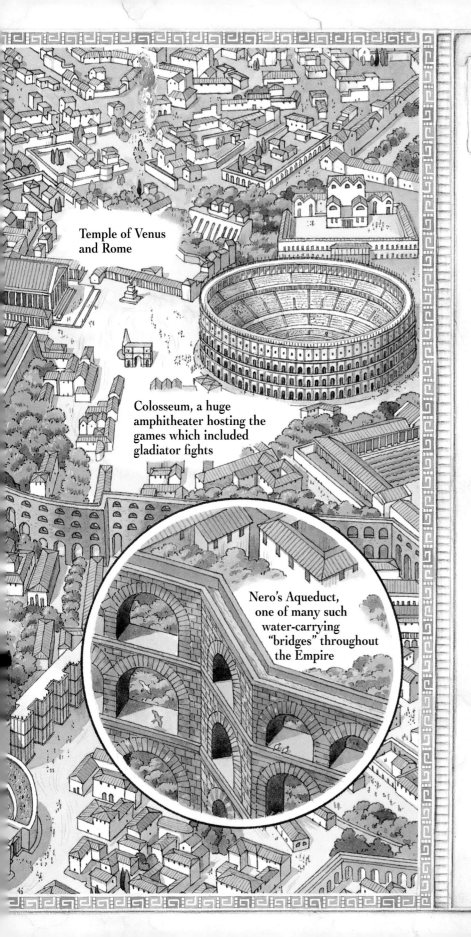

Temple of Venus and Rome

Colosseum, a huge amphitheater hosting the games which included gladiator fights

Nero's Aqueduct, one of many such water-carrying "bridges" throughout the Empire

DISCOVERY

Legend says that abandoned baby twins, Romulus and Remus, were found and brought up by a she-wolf, as shown in this statue. Later they decided to build a city. Romulus ended up killing his twin, becoming ruler of the city and naming it "Rome" after himself.

This is the Pantheon in Rome, built in 25BC. Romans built such huge dome buildings with light-weight concrete.

CITIZENS AND SLAVES

In ancient Rome, it really mattered who you were. If you were a citizen, life could be good. If you were a slave, it could be terrible. Citizens were called *cives* and non-citizens were called *peregrini*, which means "foreigners" — though some foreigners did become citizens.

Only men could be citizens, of which there were three different classes. These were patricians, *equites* and plebeians. They paid no taxes and had certain rights, such as the right to vote and join the army. Most people were plebeians — these were usually farmers and traders. The *equites* were businessmen. The richest and most respected citizens were the patricians.

Non-citizens were either provincials or slaves. Provincials lived in Roman territories, but outside Rome itself. They paid taxes, but didn't have all the rights of a citizen. Slaves had no rights at all. They either belonged to the state or to citizens.

Most Roman towns had at least one *forum* – an open-air meeting place, also used for markets.

Some patricians were patrons, or *patroni* to others.

In return for money and legal help, *clientes* gave their patrons political support.

Some *patricians* were members of the Senate and were called senators.

Senators wore togas with purple edging.

equites

plebeians

14

market stalls

Rich men and women often traveled in special covered chairs called litters.

Slaves were bought from special slave markets. Their duties included fetching and carrying.

DISCOVERY

In the time of the Roman Republic, the Senate ruled Rome. Senators were elected by citizens and, by 82BC, there were 600 of them. This bronze statue, made in the 4th century BC, is thought to be of Lucius Junius Brutus, one of the founders of the Republic.

This small disc was a tag worn around a Roman slave's neck. It doesn't give his or her name, but it does say: "Hold me so I can't escape, and return me to my master Viventius on the estate of Callistus." Not all slaves wore such tags!

15

HOUSES AND HOMES

Most Romans who lived in towns or cities didn't own their homes — they rented them. These were usually in a block of apartments called an *insula*, which normally had four floors.

Most ground floors were rented out as shops or taverns. The better apartments were directly above them, on the second floor. These had a number of large comfortable rooms. On the third floor, there were smaller, but still comfortable, apartments.

The poorest families lived on the top floor in small, one-room apartments which were often made of wood, and in very bad condition.

Life was very different for rich Romans. They usually owned a town house, called a *domus*, as well as a house in the country called a villa.

Extra rooms were often built by landlords to make more money, but many fell down.

public lavatory

a *domus*, or town house, for the rich

a typical Roman villa in the country

bath house

Grapes were often grown in the garden to make wine.

family quarters

16

an *insula* — a block of apartments

People did not cook inside their apartments. It was too dangerous!

There was no need for a private bathroom. Towns and cities had many bath houses.

wall paintings

lamp

The patterns and pictures on mosaic floors were made from tiny squares of brightly colored stone.

kitchen

walled garden

family shrine

DISCOVERY

A *domus* or villa had a family shrine, called a *lararium*, such as this one, which was dedicated to the local household gods. At engagement parties, the bride-to-be would offer her toys to the gods of the shrine as a symbol of leaving her childhood behind. The *lararium* was usually in the garden.

Some rich Romans had their villas in the middle of large country estates. Here, they could go hunting and horseriding, keep exotic pets, and receive guests in style, as well as run large farms producing food. This mosaic shows an estate in North Africa.

BATH HOUSES

Bath houses were places where people could spend the whole day relaxing, talking and even eating. They offered everything from massages and wrestling to saunas and swimming. Businessmen often held meetings there. Some bath houses had libraries in them. Romans had to pay to get in, but the entrance fee was always very low.

The first bath houses were small and private, and simply places where people went to wash. Over time, they got bigger and better. The first "public" bath house opened in AD20. By AD284, there were well over a thousand public and private bath houses.

Bath houses were open from dawn until sunset.

The *frigidarium* contained a swimming pool filled with cold water.

wrestling

snack vendors

gardens

18

The hottest room in the bath house was the *laconicum*. It was very hot and steamy like a sauna.

The *caldarium* was kept very warm, and so was the pool in its center.

library

The *tepidarium* contained a small, warm pool.

Romans washed in oil. This was scraped off with special tools called *strigiles*.

Like all rooms in the bath house, it was filled with statues, gold and marble.

Clothes were left in a cloakroom.

Both men and women used the bath houses, but at different times. This mosaic, from the Piazza Armerina villa in Sicily, shows that neither bikinis nor working out are modern inventions.

These brick "mushrooms" are, in fact, the remains of the floor supports of a Roman central heating system called a hypocaust. Hot air, heated by a furnace, spread out below the floors of bath houses and between the walls to warm the rooms. Hypocausts were also used to heat Roman villas in colder climates. These remains are at Chedworth Villa in England.

CHARIOTS AND GLADIATORS

The most popular spectator "sports" were chariot races and gladiator fights, and they were watched by thousands. They could both be very bloody, and were part of what the Romans called *ludi*, or the public games.

Chariot races were the favorite, and were held in special racecourses called circuses or hippodromes. The most famous was the *Circus Maximus* in Rome itself. These races were fast and dangerous, and many charioteers fell from their chariots and were trampled to death.

Gladiator fights were held in amphitheaters, the biggest of which could hold 50,000 spectators at once. Here, people were supposed to die. Gladiators were usually prisoners or slaves, forced to fight against each other . . . or against wild animals!

There were four types of gladiator, each armed and dressed in a different way.

A trident was like a giant fork—a three-pronged spear.

The *retarius* had a weighted net and a trident, but little armor.

A *thracian*'s shield was small and round. He didn't wear metal armor.

The emperor decided the losing gladiator's fate.

It is believed that the "thumbs-up" sign meant "live," and that "thumbs down" meant "die."

Gladiators were sometimes forced to fight wild animals instead of each other.

The *murmillo* had to fight close up, because he only had a short sword.

He was well protected with a helmet and shield, and some arm and leg armor.

The *samnite* had similar protection to the *murmillo*, but wore a different kind of helmet.

DISCOVERY

This is the remains of the Colosseum — Rome's most famous amphitheater. The floor has long since gone, showing the cells below the arena where the gladiators, prisoners and wild animals were kept before the games started.

A chariot race at the *Circus Maximus* is the subject of this carving. Chariots were built for speed and each was pulled by four horses. It was a dangerous sport and there were often accidents. Many charioteers were killed or injured.

THE THEATER

The Romans loved plays, especially funny ones. The audience didn't sit and watch in silence. There was plenty of cheering, jeering, booing and hissing, too. Sometimes fights even broke out!

The first play in Rome was put on in 240BC. It was really a Greek performance, translated into Latin — the Roman language — by a Greek named Livius Andronicus. He had once been a slave.

Soon, plays became very popular, and lots of open-air wooden theaters were built. But everyone had to stand. The first stone theater was built in 55BC and could seat 27,000 people. After that, stone theaters began springing up right across the empire.

awning pole

In hot weather, awnings could be pulled over the audience, like giant sails.

Roman theaters were shaped like a half circle.

Theaters had many entrances and exits.

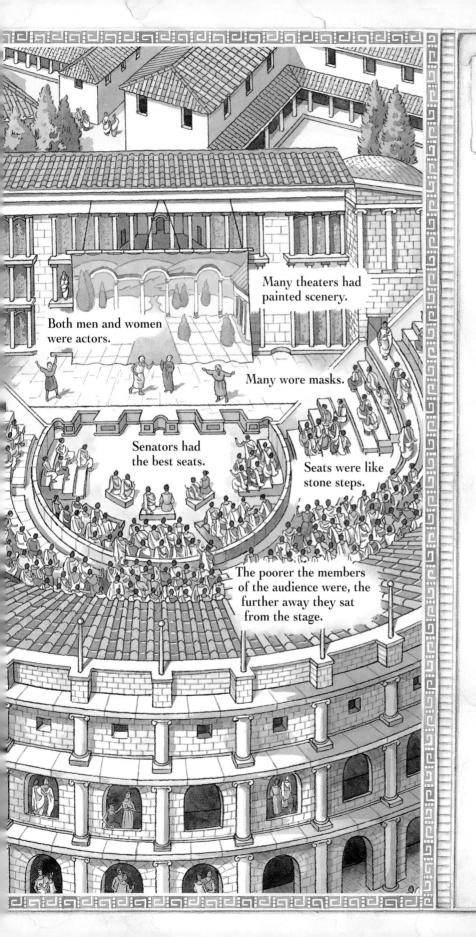

Many theaters had painted scenery.

Both men and women were actors.

Many wore masks.

Senators had the best seats.

Seats were like stone steps.

The poorer the members of the audience were, the further away they sat from the stage.

DISCOVERY

The Emperor Hadrian's villa at Tivoli is rich with beautiful mosaics. This one shows two actors' masks. Masks made it much easier for the audience to recognize familiar characters from a distance — and the same characters, such as the Smiling Fool, appeared in many plays.

This Roman theater was built in what was Gaul and is now southern France. Built at the end of the reign of the Emperor Augustus, his huge statue looks down from an alcove above the stage to this day. Plays are still performed here.

SHOPPING AND TRADE

The Romans didn't just buy from market stalls. They had streets full of shops, taverns and cafés. The shops opened directly on to the street, with only counters dividing the shopkeepers from the public. In an average shopping street, there was everything from a butcher's shop and bakery to a furniture store and jeweler's.

Many goods had to be delivered by horsedrawn carts and chariots, which caused terrible traffic jams in Rome. This was solved by banning traffic from the city during the day. All deliveries had to be made at night!

With such a large empire, Roman shops were filled with goods from all over the world, from grain grown in Britain to fine glass from Egypt. Other highly prized "goods" were slaves. They could be owned by citizens or by the government.

People lived in rented apartments above the shops.

Some shops were like modern cafés, selling food to eat in or take away.

The rich usually sent their slaves or servants to shop for them.

Plebeians and their families had to carry their own shopping.

Wine came in jars called *amphorae*.

Slaves were sold to the highest bidder.

Metalworkers sold everything from weapons to furniture.

Most items were cooked or made at the back of the shop where they were sold.

a carpenter's shop

Many of the tools used by Roman carpenters would be familiar to a modern carpenter.

DISCOVERY

Romans paid for goods with coins. They got the idea from the Greeks, in about 290BC. This coin was minted to celebrate the victory of Emperor Claudius over the Britons in AD43.

This carving shows cushions for sale in a fabric shop. Cushions added color to the home and were useful at the theater and amphitheater where the stone seats were uncomfortable.

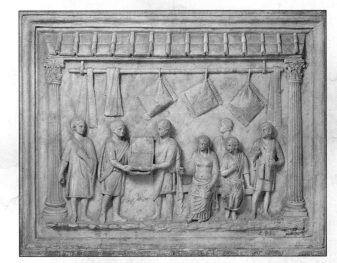

GODS AND GODDESSES

trident

Neptune (Poseidon)
God of the Sea

By the end of the 4th century AD, Rome's official religion had become Christianity after hundreds of years of Christians being persecuted. For the greater part of its history, however, Rome had its own gods and goddesses. Many of these gods were first worshipped in Greece under different names, but the Romans claimed them as their own.

For example, the Greek hero Heracles — who later became a god — was turned into the Roman hero Hercules. The Greek king of the gods, Zeus, became the Roman king of the gods, Jupiter!

Other foreign gods and goddesses kept their original names and identities. A Roman cult grew up, worshipping the Egyptian goddess Isis after Queen Cleopatra of Egypt spent time in Rome in 45BC. But other religions, such as Judaism, were not tolerated.

Minerva (Athena)
Goddess of Crafts
and War

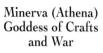

winged
sandals

Mercury (Hermes)
Jupiter's Messenger
God of Trade and Thieves

thunderbolt

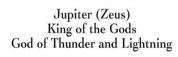

Jupiter (Zeus)
King of the Gods
God of Thunder and Lightning

Juno (Hera)
Wife of Zeus
Goddess of Women
and Childbirth

Vulcan (Hephaestus)
God of Craftsmen and Forges

26

Diana (Artemis)
Goddess of Hunting

Mars (Ares)
God of War

Dis (Pluto)
God of the
Underworld

Venus (Aphrodite)
Goddess of Love
and Beauty

Ceres (Demeter)
Mother Goddess
of Earth and
Agriculture

Bacchus (Dionysus)
God of Wine

Apollo (also Apollo)
God of Music, Healing
and Prophecy

Cupid, whose arrows
caused people to fall in
love, was seen as a much
less important god.

MOTHER EARTH

According to Roman mythology, Ceres was the Mother Goddess of the Earth, and the spirits of the woods, called wood nymphs, dedicated a special grove of trees to her.

One day, a man named Erysichthon began to chop down one of the sacred trees, despite the cries of horror from the nymphs. Every time the ax blade cut into the trunk, blood poured from the wood. But still Erysichthon chopped at the tree.

To punish him, the goddess Ceres made him forever hungry, no matter how much he ate. He sold his daughter into slavery again and again so that he could buy more and more food. (She was a shapeshifter and, once sold, could change her appearance and desert her new master every time.)

Finally, however, Erysichthon went quite mad and ate himself. Ceres was satisfied that justice had been done.

THE TEMPLES

The Romans sacrificed thousands of animals to try to please their gods, but these ceremonies took place in front of temples rather than inside them. All public ceremonies and festivals took place outside. People only went inside temples to pray in private, or to give treasure to the gods.

Temples were often filled with treasure — the prizes of war, or gifts of thanks to the gods for, supposedly, answering prayers. Priests and priestesses sometimes looked after people's own valuables, too, to keep them safe.

Different temples were dedicated to different gods or goddesses, but were all built the same way. Based on temples from ancient Greece, the front of a temple had a row of columns and often had carvings showing dramatic scenes from the god's or goddess's life.

The row of columns around a temple is called the peristyle.

Sheep, pigs, goats and doves were among the animals most frequently sacrificed.

an ox

28

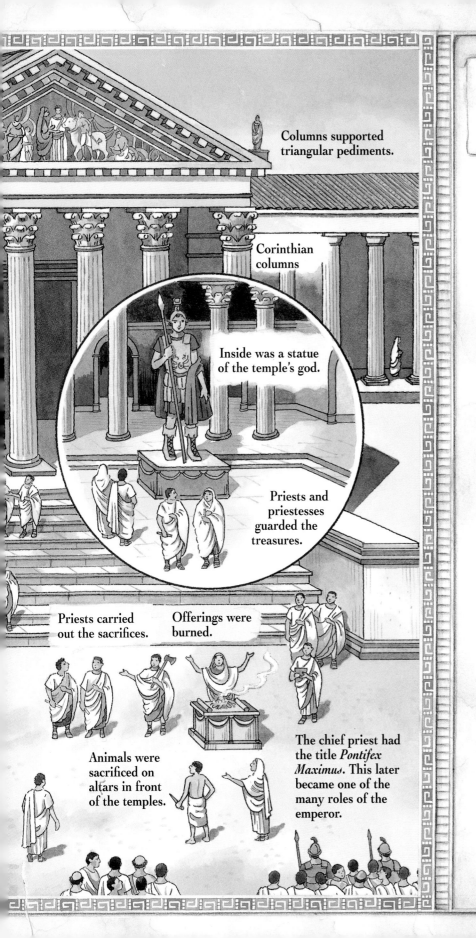

Columns supported triangular pediments.

Corinthian columns

Inside was a statue of the temple's god.

Priests and priestesses guarded the treasures.

Priests carried out the sacrifices.

Offerings were burned.

Animals were sacrificed on altars in front of the temples.

The chief priest had the title *Pontifex Maximus*. This later became one of the many roles of the emperor.

DISCOVERY

This marble head was found in the remains of a temple in London in 1954. It represents the god Mithras.

Originally worshipped in what is now Iran, Mithras became a popular god with Roman soldiers and merchants. His cult, which was strictly for men only, soon spread right across the whole empire.

Today, this building in Nîmes, France, is an exhibition center. It has been everything from a stable to a museum, but its original function is obvious. Built in the time of Augustus, this is one of the finest remaining examples of a Roman temple built in this style.

THE ARMY

Rome had one of the biggest and certainly the best organized armies in the ancient world — with as many as 450,000 soldiers in it at one time. First the Roman army invaded a country, then acted like a police force to keep Roman law.

By 100BC, most soldiers were full-time professionals paid a good wage, but life was tough. Where carts were unable to go, the soldiers did all the carrying. They were nicknamed "Marius's mules" after the commander Marius, famous for reorganizing the army. Disobedient soldiers were flogged. If serious trouble flared, every tenth soldier was executed, whether he was guilty or not.

If they weren't killed by their own side, or the enemy, full-time soldiers served for about 25 years. The only soldiers allowed to camp in Rome itself were the Praetorian Guard. Their job was to protect the emperors. Actually, they helped to murder more than one of them.

Temporary army camps, put up every night after a day's march, were always laid out in an identical way.

Army doctors were good at amputating (cutting off) damaged limbs.

Wooden stakes made a fence.

ditch

drawbridge

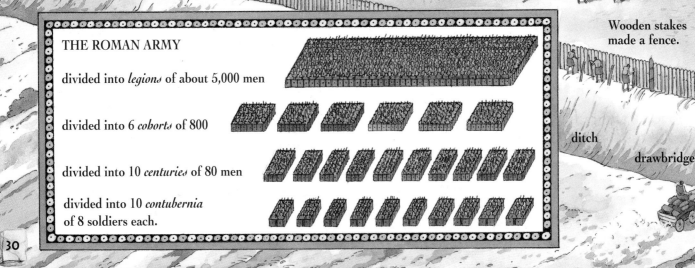

THE ROMAN ARMY

divided into *legions* of about 5,000 men

divided into 6 *cohorts* of 800

divided into 10 *centuries* of 80 men

divided into 10 *contubernia* of 8 soldiers each.

This formation, with raised shields, was called the "tortoise."

soldiers training

The general's tent was in the center.

Different officers wore different uniforms.

A centurion was in charge of each century.

plans

Every camp was laid out in the same way, so soldiers knew what went where.

A ditch was dug and the earth was used to make a defensive mound.

DISCOVERY

This Roman sword and scabbard was found in London — once the Roman city of Londinium. Parts of Britain were first invaded by the Roman army in 55BC. The carving on the scabbard is of the she-wolf who brought up Romulus.

This carving, on the triumphal arch of Titus, shows the Roman soldiers carrying off treasures, having destroyed the Jewish temple at Jerusalem in AD70. The Jews were persecuted for refusing to worship the emperor as a god, and there were many Jewish revolts against the Romans.

31

FOOD AND DRINK

In ancient Rome, what you ate depended on how much money you had. The poor lived mostly on bread and porridge made from wheat, while richer Romans ate everything from whole swans to boars' heads. With farms right across the empire producing food for Rome, there was no shortage of choice. The most popular meat was pork, sweetening came from honey, and chickens, ducks and geese were used for eggs and meat. Wine and sheep's milk were both popular drinks.

Rich Romans enjoyed feasts, and there were many special feast days in the Roman calendar. Shellfish, eggs and salad made a popular first course, usually followed by a main course of about seven dishes. A meal often ended with fruit and honey cakes.

In Imperial times, food was traditionally eaten from couches and around three sides of a table. The fourth side was left clear so that slaves could serve from there.

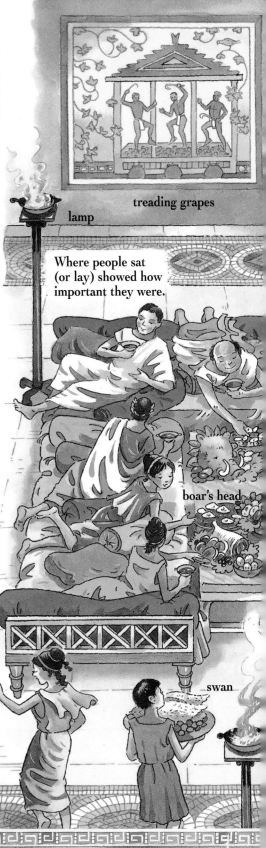

treading grapes

lamp

Where people sat (or lay) showed how important they were.

boar's head

swan

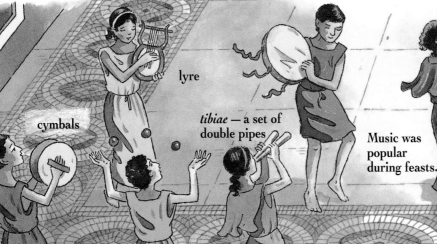

lyre

cymbals

tibiae — a set of double pipes

Music was popular during feasts.

Wall paintings often showed country scenes.

farm

Only rich people's homes had kitchens.

Food was cooked in pots on charcoal stoves.

roasting pork

Romans ate with their fingers.

Food was served with rich sauces.

fish

vegetables

meat

warmed wine

Some wines were served sprinkled with rose petals.

Farmers led hard lives compared to most people in the city. Most of the tools they used, such as these — which don't have their original handles — wouldn't look out of place in a gardener's shed today.

This huge silver serving dish is an outstanding example of the kind that rich Roman families might have owned in the 4th century AD. It is one of 34 pieces of "treasure" found at Mildenhall in Suffolk. The face in the middle represents the sea god Oceanus.

33

CLOTHES AND FASHION

Like fashion everywhere, Roman fashions changed with time, particularly clothes, jewelry and haircuts. Even beards went in and out of style!

Most men and women just wore tunics, but citizens could wear simple white togas over them. A toga was a large piece of cloth, wrapped around the body and over the left shoulder. Instead of a tunic, some richer women wore a simple dress called a *stola*. On top of these, they wore a *palla* — a colorful robe.

Rings were worn by men and women, and were usually made of gold. Women wore jewelry from head to foot: hairpins, earrings, necklaces, brooches, bracelets and anklets.

Most clothes were made from wool or linen. Rich Romans could afford expensive cotton or silk.

Fashionable men oiled and curled their hair.

toga

stola

palla

Silks from the East were brought to Rome by merchants.

Sometimes the *palla* was worn over the head.

Barber shops were popular places to meet and talk.

Customers were shaved without soap or oil.

tunic

Some women wore wigs made from their slaves' hair.

Women colored their lips with red plant dye.

earrings

cameo brooch

Women's faces, necks and arms were lightened with powdered chalk. Pale skin was thought to be beautiful.

DISCOVERY

Studying statues can be a very useful way of seeing how Roman fashions changed. A hairstyle such as the one shown in this marble head would have been made using a heated metal curling tong called a *calamistrum*.

Snake bracelets were very popular in Imperial Rome because they were thought to bring good luck. This one is made of gold and is a particularly fine example.

35

LIFE AS A CHILD

When a Roman child was born, the family performed some special ceremonies. Firstly, the baby was washed and placed at the father's feet. Then the father picked up the child, officially accepting the baby as a part of his family. Nine days later, the baby was named, and given a lucky charm, called a *bulla*, to ward off evil spirits. Many women died in childbirth. Many children died very young.

Children usually wore tunics but some boys wore a junior version of the toga called the *toga praetexta*. When a boy was 14, he would have his first shave, stop wearing his *bulla* around his neck and be given his first real toga. He'd then go to the *forum* and be made a citizen.

Only children of the wealthy were educated: boys at school, girls at home.

Some boys went on to a *grammaticus* when they were eleven.

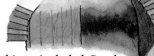

Subjects included Greek, philosophy, astronomy, history and geometry.

An early form of checkers was very popular.

Numbered knuckle bones were thrown like dice.

wooden doll

Boys from wealthy families went to the *ludus* from ages six to eleven.

Teachers were often respected Greek slaves.

the Roman numbers 1 to 10

wax tablet

13- or 14-year-olds could go on to learn public speaking. This was taught by a special teacher called a *rhetor*.

Girls learned to read, write and run a household.

Girls were often taught music.

Rich girls were taught at home.

DISCOVERY

This *bulla* is made of gold. It would have hung around the neck on a string. Originally, they were a type of leather pouch made to hold a good luck charm. Over time, they became more and more ornate, like this one. *Bullae* were worn by children who were "freeborn," that is, their fathers had to be citizens.

Children were taught Latin, the language of ancient Rome. Many English words are based on Latin ones. For example, the word "letter" comes from the Latin word *littera*. The letters on this wax tablet were written with a pointed tool called a *stylus*.

37

POMPEII—RISEN FROM THE ASHES

Walking in the streets of Pompeii today is like going back in time, thanks to the painstaking work of archeologists.

This Pompeiian mosaic carries a warning to strangers: "Beware of the dog."

On August 24th AD79, the volcano Vesuvius erupted, sending thousands of tons of lava on to the Roman port of Herculaneum. There were strong winds, and hot ash and volcanic stone were blown inland on to the town of Pompeii.

By August 26th, the whole of Pompeii was covered under 23 feet of ash and stone. At least 2,000 Pompeiians were killed. The others had fled their homes, never to return.

Over time, plants and trees grew on top of the ash and Pompeii was forgotten. For hundreds of years, farmers plowed the soil which covered the town.

AN EYEWITNESS ACCOUNT

Pliny the Younger, seventeen at the time of the eruption, was staying in Misenum (on the opposite side of the Bay of Naples) when Vesuvius erupted. He later wrote that many people believed that "this night would be the world's last" and that "there were no gods." The air was black not like "a moonless night, but the darkness of a sealed room." It was filled with "the shrill cries of women, the wailing of infants [and] the shouting of men."

A NEAR MISS

In 1593, a count called Muzzio Tuttavilla wanted fountains for his villa at Torre Annunziata. He ordered the building of an underground tunnel to carry the water supply, and his workers dug right down into Pompeii. But he thought they'd only uncovered an old Roman villa, so the town remained a secret.

UNTOLD DAMAGE

The port of Herculaneum was actually discovered before Pompeii, even though it was now under 78 feet of solid rock (since the volcanic lava had hardened). An engineer called Chevalier Alcubierre was put in charge of excavations in 1738. Unfortunately, he used gunpowder and pickaxes in an effort to find treasure. He dug tunnel after tunnel and did much more damage than good.

DISCOVERED

Once Herculaneum was discovered, interest grew in trying to find Pompeii. Alcubierre was put in charge again and, in March 1748, a number of exciting finds were made. Unfortunately, Alcubierre was as greedy as ever and caused more damage. Later, a Swiss architect called Karl Weber began carefully planned excavations. He kept accurate records of what was found and where. His work was continued by the Spaniard, Francesco La Vega.

A MOMENT IN TIME

In 1860, Giuseppe Fiorelli was put in charge of the project. It is thanks to Fiorelli that Pompeii is what it is today — a snapshot of what life was like in a Roman town in AD79. Although many other archeologists have worked on the site, right up to the present day, they were inspired by Fiorelli's methods.

THE GHOSTS TAKE SHAPE

When the hot ash covered Pompeii nearly 2,000 years ago, it trapped and killed men, women and children. Over time, their bodies rotted away, but the shapes of their bodies were perfectly preserved as holes in the ash. Fiorelli realized that, by pouring liquid plaster of Paris into these holes, he could re-create the exact shape of these people when the plaster set hard!

This plaster cast of a choking person brings the last moments of Pompeii to life. It is easy to imagine the hot volcanic ash raining down on the town.

It's not only people's bodies that have taken shape. This is a plaster cast of a hole in the ash left by the body of a Pompeiian dog, guarding its owners' home.

DISCOVERY

This bronze statue known as the "Seated Gladiator" or the "Boxer" was discovered in Rome in 1885. It looked so lifelike when it was dug up that an

archeologist said that it seemed to be a man "waking from a thousand years' sleep."

Roman roads, such as this one, were not only very straight, but also built with a slight camber. This means that they were higher in

the middle than at the sides. This way the water would run off the top, instead of collecting in big puddles.

DISCOVERING THE PAST

Archeologists are people who study the past by looking at things which have been left behind by earlier civilizations. Often they have to dig up these items first. Archeologists are the true History Detectives, piecing together clues left behind by ancient peoples. In this way, they build up a picture of how men, women and children might have lived before us. Because the Roman Empire stretched so far and wide, Roman remains can be found in many different countries throughout the world.

MARCHING ON

Once the Romans had conquered a country, they used their army to keep law and order. The legions needed to be able to march quickly from place to place, so roads were built between important locations. Roman roads are famous for being very straight, and in countries such as Britain many roads still follow the route of the old Roman ones.

DESTRUCTION AND REBUILDING

In Rome itself, many important ruins and artifacts still survive today, but thousands of items were removed over the centuries. When the troops of the great French general, Napoleon Bonaparte, occupied the city at the end of the 18th century, huge amounts of treasure were shipped to France. At the same time, though, Napoleon was interested in excavation and restoration — discovering and repairing ancient buildings.

PROTECT AND SURVIVE

Under the French, laws were passed to protect the ancient monuments of Rome. Before anyone could start digging, they needed special permission and a permit. In 1870, Rome became capital of the country we now call Italy. Hundreds of new buildings were constructed, leading to the destruction of many of the old — but there were still those who cared enough to try to protect all things ancient.

A MODERN DICTATOR

The emperors of ancient Rome were dictators. (This meant that they had total, personal control of their country. They could do what they liked.) In the 20th century, Italy — and, therefore, Rome — was ruled by a new dictator called Mussolini. He wanted to return Rome to the "glory" of the ancient times and had many modern buildings pulled down so that archeologists could try to discover and uncover more of the ancient buildings and monuments. Like many of the ancient Roman emperors before him, Mussolini was later killed by his own countrymen for his terrible cruelty.

POLLUTION

Archeologists are not only on the lookout for new finds, but also do what they can to look after existing ones. Traffic can be as big a threat to many ancient monuments as dictators or thieves. The center of Rome is full of many outstanding ancient monuments, but also millions of cars. Exhaust fumes from cars can seriously damage stonework over time. Archeologists are doing what they can to overcome these effects.

DISCOVERY

In AD113, a 98 foot column was erected to celebrate the victories of Emperor Trajan. It still stands in Rome today and is covered with relief carvings, such as these. They have given archeologists and historians very important information about life in the Roman army at that time. Here, soldiers are shown building a fort.

Although this appears to be a motorway or railway bridge it is, in fact, an ancient Roman aqueduct. This used to supply fresh water to the people of Nîmes in what is now France, from over 25 miles away.

TIMELINE

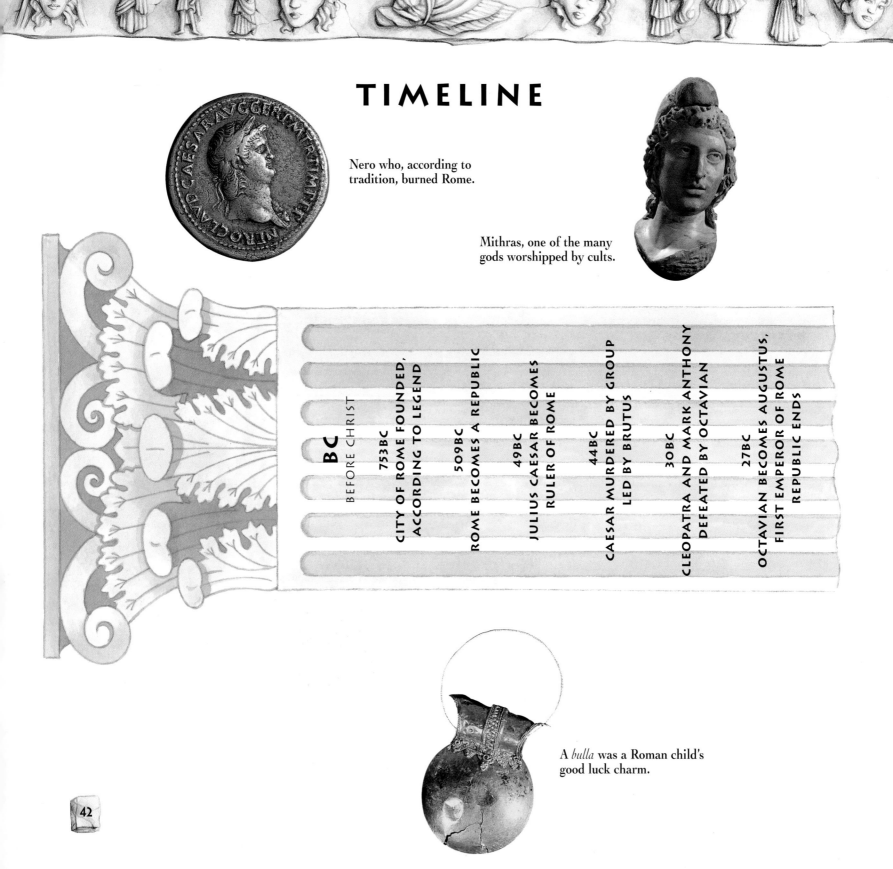

Nero who, according to tradition, burned Rome.

Mithras, one of the many gods worshipped by cults.

BC BEFORE CHRIST

753BC CITY OF ROME FOUNDED, ACCORDING TO LEGEND

509BC ROME BECOMES A REPUBLIC

49BC JULIUS CAESAR BECOMES RULER OF ROME

44BC CAESAR MURDERED BY GROUP LED BY BRUTUS

30BC CLEOPATRA AND MARK ANTHONY DEFEATED BY OCTAVIAN

27BC OCTAVIAN BECOMES AUGUSTUS, FIRST EMPEROR OF ROME REPUBLIC ENDS

A *bulla* was a Roman child's good luck charm.

The ancient Roman army conquered much of the world known to them.

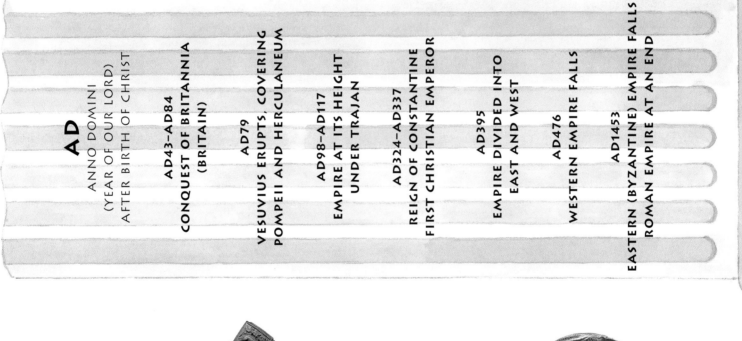

AD
ANNO DOMINI
(YEAR OF OUR LORD)
AFTER BIRTH OF CHRIST

AD43–AD84
CONQUEST OF BRITANNIA
(BRITAIN)

AD79
VESUVIUS ERUPTS, COVERING
POMPEII AND HERCULANEUM

AD98–AD117
EMPIRE AT ITS HEIGHT
UNDER TRAJAN

AD324–AD337
REIGN OF CONSTANTINE
FIRST CHRISTIAN EMPEROR

AD395
EMPIRE DIVIDED INTO
EAST AND WEST

AD476
WESTERN EMPIRE FALLS

AD1453
EASTERN (BYZANTINE) EMPIRE FALLS
ROMAN EMPIRE AT AN END

Roman relics are scattered across the globe.

Fine gold jewelry was popular with the rich.

43

KIDNAP!

A MYSTERY ADVENTURE STORY

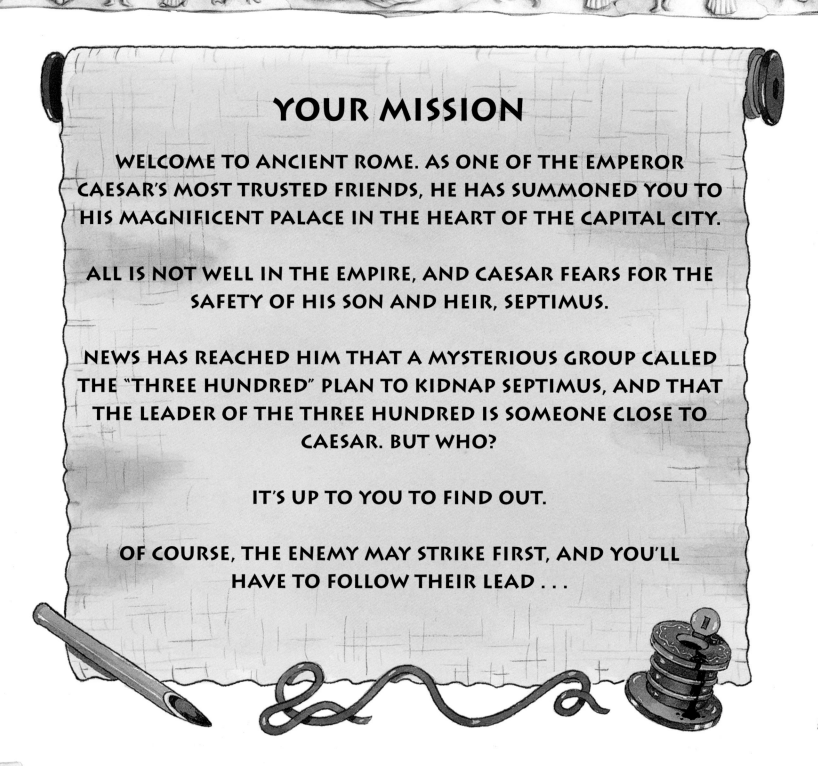

YOUR MISSION

WELCOME TO ANCIENT ROME. AS ONE OF THE EMPEROR CAESAR'S MOST TRUSTED FRIENDS, HE HAS SUMMONED YOU TO HIS MAGNIFICENT PALACE IN THE HEART OF THE CAPITAL CITY.

ALL IS NOT WELL IN THE EMPIRE, AND CAESAR FEARS FOR THE SAFETY OF HIS SON AND HEIR, SEPTIMUS.

NEWS HAS REACHED HIM THAT A MYSTERIOUS GROUP CALLED THE "THREE HUNDRED" PLAN TO KIDNAP SEPTIMUS, AND THAT THE LEADER OF THE THREE HUNDRED IS SOMEONE CLOSE TO CAESAR. BUT WHO?

IT'S UP TO YOU TO FIND OUT.

OF COURSE, THE ENEMY MAY STRIKE FIRST, AND YOU'LL HAVE TO FOLLOW THEIR LEAD . . .

HOW TO BE A HISTORY DETECTIVE

To help you solve the mystery, you will need to answer questions along the way. These can be answered by using information from the first half of this book. Simply turn to the page number shown in the magnifying glass.

For example, 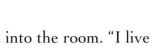 would mean that an answer lay somewhere on page 12.

These answers also earn you points, so that you can keep score. You'll find how many points an answer scores when you check yours against the answers on pages 58 and 59.

But you must do more than simply answer the questions to find out who is the kidnapper. You must look out for clues in the words and pictures, too.

By the end of the story, you should be able to say who the kidnapper is. You can find out if you're right by checking page 60. The right solution will score you an extra 20 points.

Add up all your points and find out how good a history detective you are (also on page 60).

Good luck!

YOUR MISSION BEGINS

The Emperor of all Rome stands on the palace balcony, the folds of his purple-edged toga rippling in the morning breeze. Below, the glorious city of Rome stretches out before him.

"Nowhere seems safe any more," he says, sweeping back into the room. "I live in fear of assassins."

"Then where are your Praetorian Guard, Caesar?" you ask, looking about for his bodyguards. You are alone with the Emperor, surrounded by marble pillars in this splendid room.

"I trust very few people," he insists, putting his arm on your shoulder and fixing your gaze with his eyes, "but you are one of them. Whatever is spoken here between us now must remain a secret . . . There are rumors that my son, Septimus, is in danger. I have doubled the guard around him."

Just then the doors are flung wide open, and Caesar's adviser, Optimus, hurries into the room. He gives you a quick glance and a nod of respect.

"Forgive the interruption, mighty Caesar," he says, his head bowed, "but I have terrible news. Your son, Septimus, has been seized by the Three Hundred! The attackers were swift and had surprise on their side. Six guards were killed. I've had soldiers searching everywhere. They found this. It belongs to Septimus."

What is it? **36**

You arrive with Optimus at the street where the object was found. Soldiers, led by Commander Commodus, are searching the shops and houses for the Emperor's son.

Commander Commodus strides across to Optimus. "There's no sign of Septimus, and no one admits seeing anything out of the ordinary," he says.

A shopkeeper lets out a cry. "Stop wrecking my shop!" he shouts at a soldier.

"We're here on the Emperor's business," snarls the soldier, careful not to say who they're searching for.

A boy scuttles over to you and tugs the edge of your tunic. "Not everyone here trusts soldiers," he whispers. "But I saw something. A cart heading out towards the country."

A cart? What's so strange about that? **24**

The boy, whose name is Marcus, points to the way the cart went. You turn to tell Commodus the news, but he and his soldiers are already marching off in the other direction.

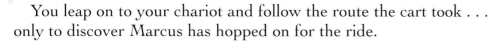

You leap on to your chariot and follow the route the cart took . . . only to discover Marcus has hopped on for the ride.

"I could be useful to you," he says. "I know many people in these parts."

You arrive outside the walls of a villa. "Look," says Marcus. "There are cart tracks leading through the archway."

You're more interested by something you've seen that looks out of place in the garden. What is it? **20**

You slip into the garden and make your way to the villa. You want to find out if Septimus is here, before going back for the soldiers. Marcus is not far behind.

"Keep out of sight!" you warn him.

You peer through a window and can't believe your eyes. The room is in chaos. Food and drink have been knocked on to the floor, and a group of people are tied up in the corner. You dash inside with Marcus, and untie them.

"Thank you!" says one. "I am Senator Titus. A small group of men calling themselves the Three Hundred came here in a cart and forced their way in. Their leader was referred to as 'Murmillo' and was dressed as one, so we couldn't see his face."

Why not? What's a *murmillo*? **21**

"They were very rough and tied us up," says Titus's wife, Faustina. "They had a boy prisoner with them."

It must be Septimus for sure! You ask Titus exactly what happened, and he explains.

"We had just come back from the bath house," he says, "and were enjoying a meal, when a group of men burst in . . .

"They shut the slaves in the sheds . . .

herded us together . . .

then they took our horses.

"Apart from the army, I have — I *had* — some of the finest horses in Rome," sighs the senator. "No wonder those swines robbed us."

"I heard the *murmillo* say something about planning to smuggle the boy somewhere under a tortoise!" cries Faustina. She pauses. "That can't be right though, can it?" she adds, doubtfully.

Yes it can. What's a tortoise? **31**

With the thanks of Senator Titus and Faustina still ringing in your ears, you leave the villa with Marcus and ride back into the city. Where to next? Perhaps the kidnappers' leader really is a gladiator. You decide to go to an amphitheater to ask around.

There are no games today, and a handful of gladiators are practicing in the deserted arena. You can hear the roar of wild animals locked in their cages.

"Who's in charge here?" you ask.

"Who's asking?" says a grey-haired man with huge bulging muscles.

"A friend of Caesar," you say.

"Then you are a friend of mine," says the man. "I am Maximus, a loyal friend to the Emperor. I train the gladiators."

Marcus gasps and points to an enormous gladiator standing behind the trainer. "He was one of the men I saw in the cart."

Before you have time to think, the vast man is running off across the dirt floor.

"Cornelius! Come back!" Maximus commands, but the giant of a gladiator keeps on running. Marcus is in pursuit, with you hot on his heels.

Cornelius runs out of the arena, between the empty seats and out of the amphitheater into the street.

"There!" says Marcus. "He went through the doorway by the *equites*." But you can see three doorways . . .

Which doorway does Marcus mean? (14)

THE ENEMY WITHIN

Dashing through the doorway, you find yourself inside a bath house . . . but there's no sign of Cornelius.

"A huge man just went into the *laconicum*," says an attendant. "There's only one way out."

There isn't a moment to lose. Which way should you go? **19**

You send Marcus to go and find some soldiers while you keep watch on the door to the *laconicum*. You grow tired of waiting and sneak inside. Hidden by the steam, you overhear a conversation.

"Someone is snooping about asking questions, Murmillo," says a deep booming voice. You're willing to bet it belongs to Cornelius. "And a boy recognized me."

"Don't worry," whispers a familiar voice. "They'll never find Septimus until it's too late."

If only you could remember whose voice it is. It's a man's . . . but whose? If only he wasn't whispering.

"Now I've been recognized as one of the Three Hundred, I'll need to hide," says the huge gladiator.

"Go to the statue of Mercury," says the man. "You'll find Claudia there. Give her today's password 'three of three hundred' and she'll hide you."

You're sure you've passed a statue of Mercury. Where was it? **26**

Just then Cornelius dashes out of the doorway past you, and slap-bang into the arms of the soldiers whom Marcus has brought into the bath house.

"That's him!" he cries. It takes four men to wrestle the gladiator to the ground.

"In here!" you shout, but the steam room is empty . . . Somehow Murmillo has slipped away unseen.

"What next?" asks Marcus.

"No time to explain," you say. "Follow me in case I get into trouble, but stay out of sight!" You hurry off to the statue of Mercury. As Murmillo had promised in the steam room, a woman is waiting beneath it. She's wearing a blue *palla*.

You say the password so she'll think you're part of the kidnap gang.

"I don't know you," she says.

You have to think quickly. "And I don't know you, Claudia," you say. "At least you know you can trust me because I know your name and gave you the password. How do I know I can trust you?"

"You have little choice," she says. "What do you want from me?"

What you really want is for her to lead you to Septimus, but she may not know where he is being held. "I need you to hide me," you say. "Cornelius has been recognized and the Praetorian Guard are everywhere."

"Sssh!" the woman insists. "You never know who might be listening."

Claudia leads you to a block of apartments. "You can hide here, tonight," she says. "The cheapest apartment is empty." Before you have a chance to ask her any more, she hurries off. Which apartment should you go to? 16

Once inside, you're relieved to find that the place really is empty. You decide to search the place for clues and don't hear the footsteps behind you until it's too late. A huge shadow looms over you and you spin around in horror to find a huge figure bearing down on you.

It's Commodus of the Praetorian Guard—the commander who is leading the hunt for Septimus.

He recognizes you. "Why are you here?" he demands. "I thought you might be a villain—one of the kidnappers, even. My men have been keeping watch on this place . . . it is believed to be a hiding place for criminals."

"Have you found Caesar's son?" you ask, hopefully.

He shakes his head.

You tell him about finding Senator Titus and Faustina tied up and about your trip to the amphitheater and what happened in the bath house.

"My men are holding the gladiator Cornelius," Commodus says. "But that still doesn't explain how you came to be here."

"I overheard the man in the *laconicum* tell Cornelius to contact a woman under the statue of Mercury," you tell him. "I found her—she was wearing a blue *palla*—and pretended to be one of the gang in trouble, and she hid me here."

"Where is this Claudia woman now?" demands the commander.

"I don't know," you admit.

The commander seems angry. "If you had come to me, one of my men could have followed her," he snaps. "She might even have led us straight to Septimus!"

Your face reddens and you hurry back to the palace to report to Caesar. There's no sign of Marcus.

"The Emperor is looking for you everywhere!" cries his adviser, Optimus. "Go to him at once."

> *Caesar*
> *We have your son. He is alive. He is well, for now. Follow our instructions and he will live. Send a representative to the Theatre of Marcellus. Have them sit in the front row of the senators' seats tonight.*
> *CCC*

Caesar is holding a scroll. "It was handed to one of the guards at the gate by a girl. She slipped into the crowd before he had a chance to grab her." You read the scroll.

Whereabouts in the theater are the senators' seats? **23**

You read the message for the umpteenth time, searching for any clues. "There's no doubt now that it's the mysterious Three Hundred who sent the letter and have Septimus," says Optimus, pointing at the note.

The letter C is Latin for the number 100, so signing the message with three Cs spells out 300.

"Do we know how the gang got its name?" you ask.

Optimus shakes his head. "I suspect they call themselves the Three Hundred to sound as if there are plenty of them," he says.

"Well, I'll use three *thousand* to crush them," fumes Caesar, "once my son is back here safe and well."

He asks you to be the one to go to the theater. You must hurry to get there for the evening performance. You arrive as the last few people are making their way to their seats.

You're obviously not a senator and you get some strange looks . . . but you're wearing Caesar's ring so no one dares argue with you. The play starts, and you wait to see what the kidnappers do next.

A man walks along to the front row and squeezes in next to you. It's Senator Titus! "I have a message for you from the Three Hundred," he whispers.

"You're one of the kidnappers!" you gasp.

He shakes his head. "No," he insists. "I'm just being used, like you are. I received a note telling me to tell the non-senator seated here to go behind the stage and wait for a woman wearing a yellow *palla* and red *stola* . . . and to hurry."

You dash behind the stage and look out for the person Titus described. Which one is she? **34**

FACE TO FACE

When you get closer to the woman in the red *stola* you recognize her. It's Claudia. "So Caesar sent you, his spy, to represent him," she sneers. "What I'd like to know is where you got our password from."

"Just tell me what the Three Hundred wants from the Emperor, so that he can get Septimus back," you say.

"Gold," says Claudia. "We want gold . . . three thousand pieces. See, we're not too greedy. Surely the life of Caesar's son is worth more than that?"

"Why make me come here to tell me this?" you ask. "You could have written your demands in your message."

"To show you that Septimus is still alive," says Claudia, "in case you had any doubts. Look over there."

You follow her gaze and there, in the distance is Murmillo — his face hidden by his helmet — standing with his hand on a boy's shoulder.

"In case you hadn't guessed, there's a sword pointing in Septimus's back," says Claudia. "Now, go back to the Emperor and tell him what we want. Have the gold ready by tomorrow afternoon. Bring it here when the theater is closed and leave it under the *tibiae*."

You watch Claudia hurrying away, then look back to where Murmillo and the boy were standing. They're nowhere to be seen.

What did Claudia mean by the *tibiae*? **32**

Just then, Marcus reappears.

"Where have you been all this time?" you ask.

"Following her everywhere," he says, nodding after Claudia. "I think I know where they've been hiding Septimus . . . and they'll probably take him back there. It's a vineyard on the outskirts of the city," he says, excitedly, and quickly explains where it is.

"You go to the palace and tell Caesar," you say, giving him Caesar's ring to get inside. "I'll go to the vineyard."

Marcus was right! You arrive at the entrance to the vineyard just as Murmillo is tying his horse to a tree. He has a firm grip on Septimus with his other hand. They step under an archway, and you follow at a safe distance.

Through the archway you find yourself in the vineyard, with row after row of vines. With Murmillo's sword pointing at Septimus's back, you daren't try to rescue the boy but, suddenly, he manages to break free and runs from his captor.

Murmillo lunges after the Emperor's son, so you leap out of hiding and launch yourself at the gang leader.

He stumbles against a tub of grape juice and drops his sword. With a curse, he manages to keep upright and moving, and dashes into a building.

Septimus is free!

With a cry of joy, he shouts "Father!" and you turn to see Caesar with Marcus and a century of soldiers pouring through the archway.

"The leader of the Three Hundred is in there!" You point at the building. In next to no time, the place is surrounded.

"My son is safe and now we have Murmillo, thanks to you and this boy, Marcus," says Caesar. You've never seen the Emperor looking so happy.

He turns to a centurion. "Search the building from top to bottom," he commands. "Check everywhere — even in the hypocaust, if it has one. Murmillo is not going to slip through our fingers now!"

What is a hypocaust? **19**

Once the building is surrounded, you step inside. The soldiers round up four men: Titus, the Senator, Commodus, the Commander, Optimus, the Emperor's adviser, and Maximus, the gladiator trainer.

One of these men is also Murmillo, leader of the Three Hundred who kidnapped Septimus. But which one is he?

Marcus appears with the *murmillo* helmet and clothing. "I found these in a pile in a corner in the other room," he says.

"I considered all of you trusted friends," sighs Caesar. "Yet one of you has betrayed me."

"Surely you do not suspect me, sire?" says Commodus. "I am here on your business, searching the area for Septimus."

"And I am here because I received another note from the kidnappers, saying that they would harm your son if I did not appear," says Titus.

"What about you, Optimus?" Caesar asks his adviser. "Why are you here?"

"The Commander sent for me in your name," he protests.

"Either you are lying, or someone tricked you!" says Commodus with a frown.

"Well, one of you four is certainly lying," you say. "But you've made a number of mistakes along the way. I already know which of you is Murmillo."

"Excellent," says Maximus, the gladiator trainer, getting to his feet. "Then, perhaps we can get this over with."

Who is the leader of the kidnap gang?

You can check your answer with the SOLUTION on page 60

TITUS

COMMODUS

OPTIMUS

MAXIMUS

ANSWERS AND SCORES

Next to each answer is a number. This is the number of points you should award yourself if you got the answer right without looking it up here in the back first. And there are extra points if you worked out who is the leader of the gang who kidnapped Septimus.

PAGES 48 & 49

- The object found by the soldiers is a *bulla* — a lucky charm worn by boys.   6 points

- It was strange to see a cart because carts are banned from the city of Rome during the day.   6 points

- That's no garden rake! That's a gladiator's trident (three-pronged spear) leaning up against the tree.   6 points

- A *murmillo* is a kind of gladiator whose head is covered with a helmet.   6 points

- A "tortoise" is a battle formation where soldiers raise their shields around them to make a protective shell.   6 points

PAGES 50 & 51

- *Equites* are people — Roman businessmen. The people in front of the door on the right have purple-edged togas, so they are senators. *Equites* aren't senators, so Marcus must have seen Cornelius go through the first doorway.   6 points

- Follow that steam straight ahead! The *laconicum* is the steam room.   6 points

- The god Mercury has wings on his sandals. A woman in a blue *palla* is standing by a statue with winged sandals in the middle doorway on page 50.   7 points

PAGES 52 & 53

- The poorest people live in the cheapest flats which are usually one room on the top floor. Claudia says the flat is empty, so it must be the top left-hand one.   6 points

- In all theaters, the senators' seats are at the front.   6 points

PAGES 54 & 55

- Although there are a number of people wearing *stolae* — some of them even red — and a number wearing yellow *pallae*, only one is wearing a red *stola* and a yellow *palla* — the woman immediately to the left of the middle pillar.　　　　　6 points

- *Tibiae* are a musical instrument also known as "twin pipes." There is a carving of *tibiae* on one of the columns behind Claudia.　　　　　6 points

PAGES 56 & 57

- A hypocaust is an underfloor heating system with spaces big enough to hide a man.　　　　　7 points

A MESSAGE TO ALL WOULD-BE HISTORY DETECTIVES

Add up your score so far, before you turn the page to find out who the kidnapper is . . .

When you've checked the solution, score an extra **10 points** if you guessed the right person.

Score **20 points** if you worked out who the kidnapper was by spotting all the clues.

SOLUTION

Senator Titus described the leader of the kidnappers as being called "Murmillo" and wearing a *murmillo's* helmet so that no one could see his face [page 49].

The whispering man in the *laconicum* — whom Cornelius the gladiator hurried off to see, and whom you couldn't see through the steam — was called "Murmillo" [page 51], so it must be him.

This rules out the gladiator trainer, Maximus, being the leader of the gang. He couldn't have left the amphitheater [page 50], reached the bath house and gone into the steam room before you did.

Caesar's adviser, Optimus, can't be Murmillo either. He has a cut on his arm which can be clearly seen [pages 48, 53 and 57]. Murmillo, though, has no cuts there [page 55]. That leaves two suspects: Senator Titus and Commander Commodus of the Praetorian Guard.

Commander Commodus claimed that he "thought you might be a villain" when he turned up in the flat used as a hideout — but he wasn't carrying a weapon, or even wearing one. It doesn't look like he was expecting trouble [page 53].

Also, when you told him about the kidnappers' contact, Claudia, you described her as "a woman in a blue *palla*" — you didn't mention her name [page 53]. Yet Commander Commodus actually refers to her as "Claudia" straight away [page 53].

Also, how did Claudia know you were Caesar's spy when you went behind the stage at the Theater of Marcellus? The last time she saw you she thought you were one of the Three Hundred. You didn't identify yourself as Caesar's representative when you went backstage. Of all the suspects, only Commander Commodus knew how you tricked her into taking you to the flat.

But how do we know that the commander is actually the leader of the Three Hundred — the man whose face is hidden by the *murmillo* helmet?

When Murmillo was escaping from you in the vineyard, he stumbled against a vat of red grape juice. You can still see splashes of juice against Commodus's legs. He is the man you're after.

BY THE WAY

As you know, the kidnap gang is called the Three Hundred, and the "CCC" they signed the note with (page 53) is the Latin numbers for 300 (page 54). It is also the initials of the three leaders of the gang: Cornelius, Claudia and (you guessed it) Commodus, which is how they came up with the name in the first place!

HOW DID YOU DO?

BETWEEN 90 AND 100 POINTS Wow! When it comes to being a History Detective, you're the very best. You're not only good at following the clues, but you worked them all out brilliantly. Well done. **BETWEEN 75 AND 89 POINTS** Excellent! You're true detective material. You worked well with the facts to solve the clues. **BETWEEN 60 AND 74 POINTS** Not bad. Not bad at all. You've got some way to go before you're a truly great detective, but you certainly know how to handle an investigation. **BETWEEN 50 AND 59 POINTS** OK, so you're not going to win any big-shot detective awards, but you're on your way to becoming a pretty good detective. Keep practicing! **LESS THAN 50 POINTS** Oh dear. A short spell at detective school wouldn't do any harm. Better luck next time.

GLOSSARY

Amphitheater — an arena for gladiator fights and wild animal shows.

Caesar — the emperor's title, originally taken from the name Julius Caesar. Each emperor decided who would become Caesar after him. Sometimes murder or political fighting prevented this.

Carthage — a city on the coast of North Africa, founded by the Phoenicians. People from Carthage were called Carthaginians, and fought in the Punic Wars under General Hannibal.

Citizens — Roman men who were born in Rome itself. They had the right to vote and to serve in the army. By AD212, all men could become citizens except for slaves.

Consuls — the most important men in the Senate. They were in charge of the business of the Senate and the army.

Dictator — an official appointed by the Senate, who held complete power over the state. A dictator was only supposed to rule for six months. Later, "dictator" referred to anyone in total personal control of a country.

Forum — a square, or other large open space, at the heart of any Roman town.

Gauls — people originally from Gaul, now called France.

Latin — the language of ancient Rome. Many modern languages — including English — contain words based on Latin ones.

Latins — a tribe of people who originally came from central Europe. They settled in what is now called Italy in about 2000BC, and were the first Romans.

Ludi — public games, sports and plays, often put on to mark special occasions such as religious festivals or great victories.

Mosaic — a picture or a pattern, made up of small pieces of colored stone or tile.

Praetorian Guard — the emperor's elite soldiers, numbering about 9,000. The only soldiers stationed in Rome itself.

Punic Wars — from the Latin word *Punicus*, meaning Phoenician. Three separate wars were fought between the Romans and the Carthaginians, between 262BC and 146BC.

Republic — a country or state governed by people elected by the people. Rome became a republic at the beginning of the 6th century BC. It became an empire when Octavian became the Emperor Augustus in 27BC.

Roman Empire — Rome and all its territories, ruled over by an emperor and sometimes referred to as Imperial Rome.

Sacrifices — animals killed and given "in offering" to the gods and goddesses.

Senate — Rome's parliament, made up of senators. The Senate was most powerful during the Republic.

Slaves — men, women and children owned by other people or by the state. In later times, some slaves were able to buy their freedom.

Toga — the main clothing of a Roman citizen. A large semi-circular piece of cloth, worn over a tunic.

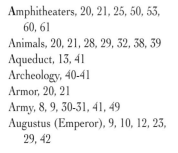

INDEX